"Better Memory Now" Series Presents:

MEDICAL TERMINOLOGY MASTERY

Proven Memory Techniques to Help Pre Med School & Nursing Course Students Learn How to Creatively Remember Medical Terms to Master Dictionary Prefix, Suffix, & Root Words

By Luis Angel Echeverria
Memory Master Champion on Superhuman
#1 Amazon Best Selling Author &
Memory Coach with AE Mind at
www.AEMind.com

YOUR GIFTS

As a bonus, you'll be the first to get my latest **Free Memory Training Videos** and Content to help you with your ongoing continued memory improvement education!

Download Here:
www.MedicalTermsBook.com/Master

You will also be able to get the Full Colored Kindle Version for Free with your purchase of the physical copy!

Just go to Amazon To Download the eBook!

LEARN MORE / CONTACT

Learn more about Luis Angel's "Better Memory Now" programs and other Memory Training material for Professionals, Students, Memory Athletes, and Everyone Else, by going to:

www.AEMind.com

SOCIAL

YT: Youtube.com/AEMindMemory
FB: Facebook.com/AEMind1
IG: AE.Mind
Twitter: @AEMind
SnapChat: AEMind

Email: MedicalTerms@AEMind.com

TESTIMONIALS

What others say about Luis Angel and The AE Mind: Better Memory Now System

Nathan Brais
Director of Student Life at Coastline College

"I just want to give a big shout out to Luis Angel Echeverria. Thank you so much for coming to our event. You're awesome, with a close to 500 students and staff here. You did 2 memory workshops for us, which the students were really impressed by, and I really appreciate you also doing our keynote address.
Luis is engaging and he's also great with students. He has a very energetic presence and I highly recommend him for any of your school events that you may be having for high school or for college group."

DANNY BELTRAN
AE Mind Memory Athlete and Student at UC Irvine.

"Joining the AE Mind team has been one of the best decisions I've ever made. **I was taught to memorize so many things without having to tear my head apart and it is so useful in academics**, *not to mention* **everyday life.** *Luis is a great mentor and coach. Without him I wouldn't be in the position I'm in now. Thanks Luis for everything!"*

KASSANDRA CEJA
AE Mind Memory Athlete and Student at UC Irvine

"Meeting Luis and joining the AE Mind Team has been a great experience. Not only did we get the chance to compete in the memory competition in New York, but we also learned skills that helped us memorize material for our academic courses. ***We also got the opportunity to learn strategies that would benefit us with our future careers.*** *Being on the team we learned lots of skills, it opened our doors to many new opportunities, we got to meet many inspiring people, and it was overall one of the best decisions I have made."*

THANK YOU

Mom!
&
Everyone Who Helped Me along the way to achieving my goals!

CONTENTS

ABOUT LUIS ANGEL

- 1st Memory Master Champion on FOX's Superhuman
- **Founder** and Main Memory Coach at AE Mind | Accelerated Empowered Mind
- **Competed** in the USA Memory Championship

- **Was the Youngest American** to Compete in the World Memory Championship with TEAM USA
- **Memorize: 120 Digit Number in 5 Minutes,**
- **Coached the AE Mind Memory Team** to a 1st Place Medal in the Numbers event at the USA Memory Championship
- **Started AE Mind Memory Clubs** in Los Angeles High Schools and in Universities such as UC Irvine and UC Santa Barbara.
- **Speaker** for Schools, Organizations, and Companies to help students and professionals have a "Better Memory Now"
- **Author and Creator of the AE Mind:** *Better Memory Now Series*

CONTRIBUTION

As someone who grew up in government-subsidized housing, on food stamps, and in an area with a lot of gang activity (never participated, but witnessed a lot of it around him), Luis Angel knows what it's like to have to go through struggle in life.

That's why Luis Angel loves contributing to help make the lives of those in need better in whichever way that he can.

GIVE BACK TUESDAY

Along with Living Waters and Countless of Amazing Volunteers, Luis Angel helps feed the homeless and families in need every Tuesday in the City of Santa Ana in Southern California.

FEED FAMILIES EVENT

Luis Angel has also partnered with Dion Jaffee, Bell High School, and several friends who donate to the cause to Feed Families every year for Thanksgiving!

A portion of the proceeds from the AE Mind Better Memory Now Live Events, Courses, and Books goes to continuing our Contribution Efforts!

Thank You In Advance for Your Contribution to the Cause!

FOREWORD

Dr. Feibi Liu PHD/PA | Founder of Skin Perfect Pro
www.FeiBiLiu.com

One of the pains of a medical education, as I can remember, is the countless hours staying up and all-nighters studying medical terminology. I always wondered if there was a better way to learn other than just rote memorization.

Now there is. Luis Angel's Medical Terms Book!

It's simple to understand, easy to apply, and works immediately. Luis used the best and latest techniques in memorization and applies it to help you master medical terminology. By applying this, you will find that your study time in rote memorization will be cut in half and your recall for the meaning of the word will be three times faster. This book will help you score higher in tests and the principles you will be able to apply in other areas of your study.

I've known Luis as a friend for many years and have seen him excel in his achievements and grow in his mastery of memory.

This is largely due to Luis Angel's incessant desire for mind growth and personal development. I have seen Luis go from an unknown to gathering a large following on YouTube, speaking on topics of memory, mind growth, success, finances, motivation and leadership. He even began to coach local high school academic decathlon teams for memory. I also had the pleasure to watch Luis win the title Super Human and awarded $100,000 prize for his memory skills on a Fox national televised show.

If you are reading this book, and are learning from Luis Angel, I have no doubt that you will get the extra edge you need to compete in your medical program. Your classmates won't understand how you have such a great memory and will just think you are a genius. But more seriously, it will require hard work for you to succeed in anything you do. All Luis did is remove the hard from the hard work. He has made it easy for you to win. You will find this to be the best training, the best technology, and you will immediately see a result and benefit.

I wish I had this book during my medical program. It would have saved me countless hours of study and my recall speed would have tripled. If you follow the strategies in these pages, you will be elevated to a whole new level. I highly recommend this book. Enjoy!

Dr. FeiBi Liu

Intro

LET'S MAKE LEARNING, FUN AGAIN

INTRO

Hi Billy/Jane (hopefully I meet you someday so that I can call you by your real name)!

I'm so happy that you took the time to invest in yourself by getting the Medical Terminology Mastery Book! I promise to deliver massive value into your life by teaching you the essential skills necessary to master the art of memorizing any medical term that you come across. Whether it is in a dictionary, glossary, or book that you're reading, you will be able to take any vocabulary word and creatively memorize it's meaning.
Because of the fact that you are engaging several components of your brain when you use the AE Mind Method of memorizing and learning information, you will notice that your ability to retain information will also skyrocket!

Your brain learns best in pictures.
It remembers information better when it can see that information.

There is this myth out there that as we get older we must become "sophisticated" learners and only read 10,000 page books full of 5 point font text from cover to cover. This is non-sense. Think back to your preschool and kindergarten years. See yourself in that classroom. Remember when Mrs. Smith used to gather everyone around in a semi-circle, pulled out the book full of fun pictures with one-line text at the bottom of the page, and began to read to us with enthusiasm. Remember how you were totally connected with the story and couldn't wait for her to turn the page to find out what was going to happen with the green eggs and ham. This is because it was an engaging story with a lot of visuals to help our brains stay focused.

Learning doesn't have to be a boring chore that we do. We must revert back to our childhood days of learning in a fun and creative manner in order to enjoy the art of retaining knowledge very easily. I created this Medical Terminology Mastery Course to help you do just that. We are going to have fun with the process of learning new information.

WHAT MAKES LUIS ANGEL QUALIFIED?

Before learning to memorize things quickly and becoming the 1st Memory Master Champion on the FOX Hit Show, SUPERHUMAN, my ability to retain info was horrible. I'm talking about, it would be 4PM and I wouldn't be able to recall if I had even eaten for the day. At school, I was failing my classes left and right. I got kicked out of a semester in college because I had such lousy grades.

Check this out. I'm sure that this has never happened to you; I used to sit down, open up my book, start going down the lines of text, turn the pages, and about 10 minutes in, I would look up and have absolutely no clue what the context of what I was reading was about. My mind would constantly wander off into la la land thinking about if the Lakers were going to win that night or if that cute girl from 3rd period liked me. I couldn't focus or concentrate and my retention skills were not optimal at all.

After going to see a doctor and presenting him with my symptoms for my memory problems, he told me that I had ADD or Attention Deficit Disorder. This is when I sought after help for my focus and memory issues.

I turned to my friend, Dion, who told me about a memory guy he once saw on stage memorizing a ton of stuff in a matter of minutes. He told me his name, Ron White, and I immediately bought his memory course. I went through it and quickly implemented what I learned into my studies.
I went from failing and getting kicked out of college to getting straight A's because of what I learned from my memory mentor and from other mind empowering books and events that I was consuming the knowledge of. My life was completely turning around and I was becoming more confident at my ability to learn quickly.

I have since gone on to compete all over the world in Memory Championships. I have collected Gold Medal Positions in events at these competitions and have even coached others to do the same. And as I mentioned before, I also became the 1st ever Champion as the Memory Master on the FOX show, SUPERHUMAN.

In all of these competitions, we as memory athletes must memorize thousands of pieces of information ranging from numbers and names, to images and vocabulary words. We have a matter of minutes to memorize as much as we possibly can. For example, at the World Memory Championship, I memorized and perfectly recalled a 120-digit number in under five minutes. On SUPERHUMAN, I had to memorize over 500 pieces of information the same day that I was tested on it. I got all of the questions correct and took home the grand prize later that night.

Now I teach students in high school and college how to take these memory techniques that have done wonders for me, and use them to learn their school material.

Recently at one of my Better Memory Now Workshops, I teaching a group of medical students how to memorize medical terminology. They were stunned at how powerful and fun it was to learn the terms using what I was teaching them.

"I love this because it helps me be creative with learning the words for my exams" said one of the students.

This is what gave me the idea to sit down and put this book together. I wanted to write a book that was going to help medical students spend less time hammering away at their flash cards using old school methods of rote memorization, and spend more time enjoying their time at school because they had already learned all of their medical terms at a fraction of the time.

My last book, "How to Remember Names and Faces," became an International Best Seller in the First Week and many individuals came to me and thanked me for putting the book out there. It relieved the problem that people had of forgetting names. It did that by putting those reading the book through a journey of practicing the memorization methods with over 500 faces. It wasn't laid out in a way where I told stories the entire book or just fed them with a bunch of theoretical ideas of how the techniques worked. I laid out the book in a way where the reader could progressively get better at remember the names of the people that they met by creatively practicing the techniques that I taught them through hundreds of examples.

That's the way that I have formatted this Medical Terminology Mastery Book as well. It's essentially a course to take you from principles and ideas to help you become a walking medical terminology dictionary if you put what I teach you into practice.

So let's get you started on the right foot.

GETTING STARTED RIGHT

Remember that this entire process is going to be a partnership.
I have gone to many seminars and read many books where the speaker or author does a one-way interaction with the audience and expects them to be experts in that topic when they're done.

That's not how accelerated learning works.

At every single one of my seminars or events, whether I'm teaching a group of thousands of people or just doing a one-on-one training, the way that I teach is very interactive. I teach you how to be a creative story teller in order to memorize information through my own examples, and then you go ahead and create your own stories to help you memorize new material.

So get ready to stretch your mind. Be like a parachute and allow your mind to work by being open to the ideas presented in this book. They have been tested all over the world by the best memorizers and they simply work when I applied correctly.

HONEST REVIEW

I love seeing the transformation that people go through when they learn this system, and I would be extremely grateful if you helped contribute to that transformation.

When you get a chance, if you could take about a minute or two to go to the Medical Terminology Mastery Book Page and leave a Review, you will truly be helping to improve the lives of thousands of students who struggle with learning medical terms.

Thank You in Advance!

Other than that, let the show begin!

Enjoy, and Much Success on your journey to have an
AE Mind!

SOURCES FOR DEFINITIONS

I crossed referenced several sources for the most accurate definitions and meanings for each one of these medical terms. They are as follows:

-Farlex Partner Medical Dictionary © Farlex 2012
-Mosby's Medical Dictionary, 9th edition. © 2009, Elsevier.
-American Heritage® Dictionary of the English Language, Fifth Edition. © 2011
-McGraw-Hill Concise Dictionary of Modern Medicine. © 2002
-Collins Dictionary of Medicine © Robert M. Youngson, 2005

Thank you for understanding.

Now Let's Have Some Fun!

Section I

THE AE MIND SYSTEM

THE AE MIND MEMORY SYSTEM

When it comes to learning new information using the memory techniques that the top memory athletes from around the world use, you must start to reprogram your brain to learning the way that it did as a young student.

I like to tell my students that
The Key to MEMORIZATION is VISUALIZATION

As a young student we learned best in story form, so we must become Creative Story Tellers when it comes to learning new material.

For example, I want you to picture this:
See a kind, loving, tail wagging every time he sees you, Siberian Husky pup. See that puppy caring for you and being very nice, never causing any trouble. That husky is always by your side licking your face every chance that he gets.

So as a reward, you give little Russel (I like to give random names to people and things) a thick envelope which you have stuffed with a treat.

Your husky, Russel, is so extremely happy to get it that he immediately tears it open and out pops out a juicy bone. He starts to salivate and without hesitation bites into it.

Okay let's pause here for a bit.

What just happened?

Well you're probably saying, dang it Luis, I want a Siberian Husky puppy now. But the story was not to entice you to go out and get a new dog, it was to show you the power of creative story telling when it comes to learning new information.

The main takeaways from the story are the Bone, Envelope, and Being Kind Hearted. The bone inside of the envelope represents the word BENEVOLENT. The definition of benevolent is, to be well meaning and kind. The puppy being nice and kind to you represented the definition.

This is essentially what we have to do in order to memorize any word and its meaning.

We take the Word and turn it into a Picture, then we take the Definition and turn that into a Picture so that we can link the two together to create a story.

That's it! Magic right?

Not really because all that we are doing is taking information that we already have in our minds and linking it to the new information that we want to learn. That is the secret of accelerated learning. Our brains are wired to learn faster when we do this.

Way back in the day, before we had writing utensils, in order for our forefathers to transfer knowledge on to the next generation, they would tell the kids very captivating stories and metaphors. They didn't know this back then, but the reason why knowledge was more easily absorbable using this method instead of just laying out facts and having the kids repeat the information thousands of times, is because multiple areas in the brain are activated when they are receiving a story. Their ability to stay focused and pay attention skyrockets when they could see, hear, feel, touch, and taste the information.

Taste? Can we really taste information?

Many times, our unconscious mind cannot distinguish between what is real and what is make belief. It is up to our conscious mind to tell it what to believe to be true or false.

I want you to play with me for a moment and imagine this:

Picture yourself right now in your kitchen. See yourself standing barefoot in front of the refrigerator. As you're standing there, feel how cool the floor feels as the transfer of energy is happening between the soles of your feet and the cold floor. Listen to the sound that the refrigerator motor is making as it's cooling the food inside of it. Look around and see, hear, and smell anything that you notice near you.

Now, reach out your arm and grasp a hold of the handle on the refrigerator door. Make that hold firmer. Tug on the handle until you pry the door open and as you do that listen the sound that the door makes as the magnetic strips holding the door shut are pulled away from each other. Now feel the cool breeze that passes past your body as you open the door. Take another nasal breath to notice that air and smell going inside of your nostril.

Next, I want you to see a lemon sitting on one of the shelve inside of the fridge. Go ahead and take hold of it. Throughout this next process take notice of all of your senses. Pull the lemon out of the fridge and close the door. Imagine yourself walking over to the cutting board where you place the lemon on top of it. Grab a knife and slice the lemon into several wedges. Feel the juices of the lemon flow down your fingers as you take a wedge and bring it up close to your mouth.

With the lemon here, I want you to smell the scent of that wedge, bring it closer to your lips, and sink your teeth into it as you suck on the lemon juice.

How does that taste? Did you notice the sensation of your cheeks clinching because of that sour taste?

How real did that feel?

Again, our brain works best when it uses as many senses as possible to capture the new information that it is being presented to it.

When I memorized a 120 digit number in a few minutes at the World Memory Championship, all that I was doing was creating a bunch of miniature stories that included a multitude of senses very quickly. Then when I wanted to recall that number, I simply reviewed the stories in my mind and translated the visual triggers back into the sequence of numbers. (I dive deeper into how to memorize numbers, names, cards, and other material in my **Better Memory Now** book)

We do that same thing with the medical terms that we will be learning about and memorizing.

To recap, here is the formula to learn the meaning of any word:

Word = Picture A
Definition = Picture B
Pic A + Pic B = Story

If you want to memorize the sequence of information such as a list in order, you need to use the 3 Step AE Mind Memory System.

We won't spend too much with this method in this book, but I still think that it is important to know and understand because you will find uses for it as you study your school material.

LOCATION METHOD

The three steps are as follows:

1. Location
A place to store the information

2. Visualize
Convert the information into an image and visualize it on the location

3. Review
Go over the Visual that you created in order to store it into your long-term memory.

Let's start off by going over the Location aspect of this process and what exactly would make for a great storage space.

"Tell me and I forget. Teach me and I Remember. Involve Me and I Learn."
-Benjamin Franklin

LOCATION

At the Australian Memory Championship, I received the Gold Position for memorizing and perfectly recalling the correct order of a shuffled deck of cards in 2 Minutes. The way that I did that was by imagining myself in my mom's house and placing the stories that I was creating a long a route. So I placed a Lion eating Diamonds (5 of Hearts and Ace of Diamonds), on the couch. On the table, I pictured a Scooby Doo driving a Tesla Car (2Spade + 7Diamond). I did this until I had all 52 cards memorized on locations in my mom's home.

Let's create a few locations to help you out with this process.

I already primed your mind earlier to help you out with this step. Since we were already in your kitchen, let's start there. Imagine like your back in your kitchen. I want you to choose 5 things in the kitchen and number them from 1-5 going clockwise. Meaning if the fridge is the first one, then what's the next item to the right of the fridge?

Here is an example of my 5 spots in the kitchen:

1. Cabinet
2. Sink
3. Toaster
4. Oven
5. Fridge

Go ahead and write out your 5 locations right now.

1. _____
2. _____
3. _____
4. _____
5. _____

Perfect. Now that you have done that, let's move on to Step 2. The fun

VISUALIZE

You got a taste of how this step works earlier, and this is where all of the "magic" happens. When you create more mental locations and expand to other rooms in your home, this magic will happen in the bedroom as well. Cheesy, I know.

So let me give you a list of 5 words to memorize and we're going to create a story with each one on your 5 locations from your kitchen.

1. Banana
2. Dynamite
3. Water
4. Computer
5. Samurai

Now let's go ahead and create stories on the locations with these words. I want you to add a lot of action to these stories to make them more memorable.

1. Picture a pile of bananas on your first location. For me it's the cabinet so I would see a banana tree growing out of the cabinet and I'm getting all of the bananas into a pile.

2. On your second location see Dynamite. I would see a myself blowing up the sink with dynamite.

3. On the third spot, picture water covering that area. So I would see a flood of water coming out of my toaster.

4. The fourth word is computer. Attach that to your fourth location. I would myself shoving a computer into my oven seeing it heat up inside. What do you see on your fourth spot?

5. On your 5th location in your kitchen, visualize a samurai doing something to that location. I would see a samurai slicing up my fridge trying to get inside of it because it wants some lemons.
You have them all locked in? Perfect! Let's do a quick review.

REVIEW

This is extremely important. If you want to take any new information that you learn from short term memory into your long term memory, you must review.

Without looking at the list, write down all 5 words that we just memorized. All that you have to do is visualize yourself in your kitchen and walk around each locations retrieving the images that we placed there.

1. _____
2. _____
3. _____
4. _____
5. _____

Now let's see how you did.

1. Banana
2. Dynamite
3. Water
4. Computer
5. Samurai

How was that?

Did you get them all correct?

Remember that the stronger the action between the picture and the location, the easier it is going to be for you to recall the information.

Also, spaced repetition is the mother of all learning.

THE IMPORTANCE OF REVIEW

I've memorized and perfectly recalled hundreds of numbers in a matter of minutes in memory competitions. Most of those sequences, I wouldn't be able to tell you what they were today. Why? Because I didn't review that list of numbers past the day of the competition. I was telling my brain that the information that I was memorizing at that giving point in time was not going to be relevant in the future. So I forgot it after I recalled it that day.

You've heard the old saying, "use it or lose it."

If you don't review the information, you will forget it or it will be much tougher for you to recall it when you really need to. Like in an important exam.

The process that I teach you here will help you to condense the amount of time that you spend looking over the information but that doesn't mean that you will look at something once and it is automatically uploaded into your long term memory forever. You must go over it in a spaced period of time manner in order to hold on to that info.

Next time you see me, ask me to say the first few hundred digits of Pi out loud both forwards and backwards.

I'll say sure. Close my eyes. Take a deep breath in through my nose and exhale softly out through my mouth as you see my shoulders start to slump down for a bit before coming back up (this is a Relaxation and Focus exercise that I go over in my Better Memory Now Book). I will then stick my arms out a bit and start doing some Tony Stark type of movement with my hands swiping left and right and scribbling into thin air as I say:

3.14159265358979323846264338327950288419716 9... so on and so forth.

Or ask me what the atomic number for any element on the periodic table of elements is, and I'll instantly give you the answer. 47 is Silver, Beryllium is 4, Carbon is 6, the 50th element is Tin... Again, this is all from memory.

Now I don't do that just to brag or show off, I do it to show you the power of the memory techniques when applied in the manner that I teach you.

So what is the difference between what I memorize in a memory competition and what I learn in an education setting?

The difference is obvious. I actually care about the information and want to hold on to it for a longer period of time when it comes to learning educational material. When I'm training for a memory competition, I want to erase the information that I memorized as quickly as possible so that I could reuse the mental locations for another set of numbers, cards, or vocabulary words.

The key element for anyone to be able to retain information for a long period of time is to Review!

So in order to forget the information that I memorized in a competition setting, I just don't review that info past the recall time in the competition.

When I want to remember something such as math formulas, vocabulary words, or someone's name, I make sure to review that information in a spaced period of time.

Meaning I'll use the Visualization Technique to Memorize the information the first time around and then I'll review the info later that day, the next day, and a few days afterwards as well.

Reviewing = Long Term Memory.

In the book "The Other Brain," Dr. Douglas Fields talks about how when we review something, brain cells called glial cells help support the neurons to fire off much more quickly the next time that you want to retrieve that information. More specifically, these glial cells shoot off something called myelin onto the neurons when they send electrical signals down the axons and then the terminals shoot off neurotransmitters to the receiving end of another neuron (the dendrites).

Oligodendrocyte

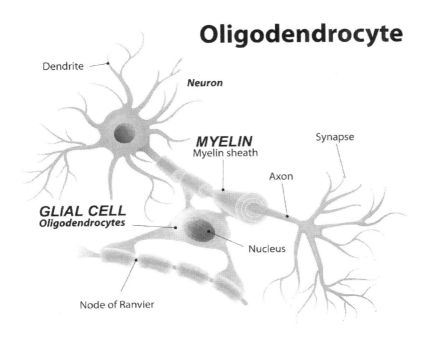

Let me explain the importance of this process through a metaphor.

As you know from reading the Intro section, I used to work for a satellite TV company. My job was to install the customer's cable and make sure that everything was running smoothly before I left. Meaning they needed to be able to see their favorite TV channels and shows before it was time for me to pack up and go to my next job.

The way that they received a pretty HD picture on their TV set was because the cable connected to the back of the receiver box was getting a digital signal coming from the satellite dish that converted another signal coming from the actual satellites floating hundreds of miles up in space.

Amazing, I know!

So what carries this electrical signal from the satellite dish, through the cable, and onto the receiver? It's a copper wire only about a few millimeters thick. It's probably as thick as an unfolded paperclip.

So why is it that the actual cable that you see hooked up to the back of your

TV cable box is much thicker than what it should be? This is because in order for the signal to flow smoothly and in a quick manner from one end to the other without getting any signal loss, the copper wire needs to be wrapped with insulation. There are actually several layers of insulation, as you see below.

I've had to go to hundreds of troubleshooting service calls at customers' houses during my stint as a cable installer, and one of the biggest problems was that the dog had chewed up the cable. They had cut through the insulation, leaving the copper cable exposed and not allowing the electrical signal to reach the cable box.

Now with that knowledge in your brain, let's apply this to how our neurons work.

Imagine that the axon, which carries the electrical signal, is the copper cable. The insulation is the myelin that wraps around the axon.

Without any or perhaps just a thin layer of myelin, the neurons don't fire off as effectively and efficiently as they should. However, when you repeatedly fire off those neurons by reviewing the information that you want to memorize and learn, the glial cells pick up on that and send myelin to wrap around the axon.

Again, Reviewing = Long Term Memory.

As an FYI, did you know that when they were looking at Albert Einstein's brain, the neuroscientists couldn't see any size difference between his brain and an average brain?

What they did see that was different was the amount of white matter in his brain. The white matter is the myelin that wraps around the neurons. He had a lot more white matter than the average human brain.

Albert Einstein was known to visualize or create thought experiments in his mind when he wanted to solve a problem.

This is just something to consider when going through this process of Visualizing in order to Memorize.

Now that you know the memorizing systems, let's put this into practice.

MASTERFULLY MEMORIZE ANY MEDICAL TERM

Now obviously I don't have all of the medical terms here. For me to be able to fill the entire lexicon of med terms with my stories and metaphors, would require an entire book shelf to fit this 20,000-page book in.

So instead, I have added the top Prefixes, Suffixes, Root Words, and also gave you plenty of examples of how you can take what I teach you here and apply it to every subject matter on your road to Nursing or Medical School.

As you will see, in certain situations I will use extra images to help me recall a letter or a portion of the word or definition. I have created pre-determined images for every letter from A through Z.

I have included those pictures here:

Alphabet Pictures

A = APPLE
B = BALL
C = CAT
D = DOG
E = ELEPHANT
F = FROG
G = GOLFBALL
H = HAND
I = IGLOO
J = JACK
K = KANGAROO
L = LION
M = MAT

N = NAIL
O = ORANGE
P = PICKLE
Q = QUEEN (CROWN)
R = ROSE
S = SNAKE
T = TOWEL
U = UMBRELLA
V = VIOLIN
W = WATER
X = XYLOPHONE
Y = YOYO
Z = ZEBRA

Section II

PREFIXES

PREFIXES

Here are some important Prefixes that you need to learn as you move forward in your medical and/or nursing field of study.

Be aware that these are my own stories and I would highly encourage you to create your own stories and visuals to help you learn these medical terms.

You will have a higher probability of near perfect retention if you create the stories yourself and you do spaced repetition.

The Memory Sequence will be as follows for the words:

Prefix = Picture A
Meaning = Picture B

Picture A + Picture B = Story

a-, an- = apple with ant
without = missing something inside

Story

An Ant cut the Apple open and was missing its core.

Term Use
anorexia = a lack or loss of appetite
[Mosby's Medical Dictionary, 9th edition. © 2009, Elsevier.]

----

ab- = abdominal area
away from = pushing away

Story

The guy was showing off his 6 pack abs and you pushed the abs away
from you.

Term Use
abaxial = lying outside the axis of any body or part
[Farlex Partner Medical Dictionary © Farlex 2012]

ambi- = apple with bambi (deer)
both = both

Story

An apple riding two bambis (deer)

Term Use
ambidextrous = having equal facility in the use of both hands
[Farlex Partner Medical Dictionary © Farlex 2012]

----

atmo- = hat + ammo
steam = steam

Story

Hat throwing ammo inside of a steam room

Term Use
atmolysis = Separation of mixed gases by passing them through a
porous diaphragm, the lighter gases diffusing through at a faster rate.
[Farlex Partner Medical Dictionary © Farlex 2012]

ante- = ant tea
in front of = in front of (action)

Story

Ant pointing to tea in front of him

Term Use

antecardium = the area on the anterior surface of the body overlying the heart and the lower part of the thorax.
[Medical Dictionary, © 2009 Farlex and Partners]

----

anti- = ant + tie
against = fighting against

Story

Ant was fighting against a tie

Term Use

antibody = an immunoglobulin produced by B-lymphocytes in response to bacteria, viruses, or other antigenic substances. An antibody is specific to an antigen.
[Mosby's Medical Dictionary, 9th edition. © 2009, Elsevier.]

apo- = apple with pole
away from = action of staying away from

Story

Ape is mad at the pole so it's staying away from it

Term Use
apochromatic = Free from spherical and chromatic aberrations.
[Medical Dictionary, © 2009 Farlex and Partners]

----

auto- = automobile
self = self-driving

Story

The automobile car is self-driving around town

Term Use
autecic = Denoting a parasite that infects, throughout its entire existence, the same host.
[Farlex Partner Medical Dictionary © Farlex 2012]

bi- = bicycle
two = two wheels

Story

Bicycle has two wheels

Term Use
biarticular = to divide into joints having two joints.
[Mosby's Medical Dictionary, 9th edition. © 2009, Elsevier.]

----

brachy- = brick
short = shorty

Story

Brick was a shorty and couldn't reach the high wall

Term Use
brachydactylic = an abnormal shortness of the fingers and toes
[American Heritage® Dictionary of the English Language, Fifth Edition. © 2011]

cata- = cat + apple
reverse = walking backwards

Story

Cat was walking backwards and ran into an apple

Term Use
cataplasia= degenerative reversion of cells or tissue to a less differentiated form
[American Heritage® Dictionary of the English Language, Fifth Edition. © 2011]

----

circum- = circus + gum
around = wrapped around

Story

Circus was wrapped around with gum

Term Use
circumanal = surrounding the anus
[Farlex Partner Medical Dictionary © Farlex 2012]

con- = ice cream cone
together = joining together

Story

Placed ice cream together on top of the cone

Term Use
concentric = describing two or more circles that have a common center
[Mosby's Medical Dictionary, 9th edition. © 2009, Elsevier.]

----

contra- = conch shell + trap
opposed = opposed (action)

Story

The conch shell and mouse trap were opposed to being near each other

Term Use
contraception = prevention of conception or impregnation
[Farlex Partner Medical Dictionary © Farlex 2012]

de- = letter "D"
remove entirely = take away a section, like a backwards "C"

Story

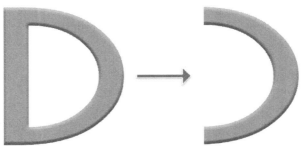

Removed the long part of the letter "D" and now it looks "C"

Term Use

decapitation = removal of a head
[Farlex Partner Medical Dictionary © Farlex 2012]

---

di- = die (dice)
two = two

Story

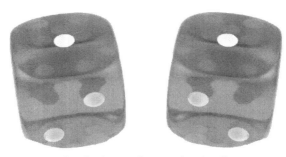

I rolled two dice and got a 2

Term Use

dimorphic = In fungi, a term referring to growth and reproduction in two forms: mold and yeast.
[Farlex Partner Medical Dictionary © Farlex 2012]

dia- = sun with sombrero *(Dia means day in Spanish. I normally use a Mexican sombrero to let me know that I'm using the Spanish version of the image that is associated for that word)*
apart = tearing apart

Story

The sun is tearing itself apart

Term Use
diactinism = Having the property of transmitting light capable of bringing about chemical reactions
[Farlex Partner Medical Dictionary © Farlex 2012]

----

dorsi- = door see (glasses)
back = back

Story

Back was leaning against the door with glasses

Term Use
dorsispinal = relating to the back and spine
[Medical Dictionary, © 2009 Farlex and Partners]

dys- = dis song

bad = bed

Story

He dissed him in his rap song because his bed was difficult to make

Term Use
dyspnea = difficult, labored, or gasping breathing; inspiration, expiration, or both may be involved
[Mosby's Dental Dictionary, 2nd edition. © 2008 Elsevier, Inc.]

----

ec- = egg
out of = taking inside out

Story

Taking the yolk out of the egg

Term Use
ecbolic = causing the pregnant womb to contract and expel its contents
[Collins Dictionary of Medicine © Robert M. Youngson, 2005]

em- = M&M
on = on top

Story

Stacking M&M on top of each other

Term Use

embolism = Obstruction or occlusion of a vessel by an embolus
[Medical Dictionary for the Health Professions and Nursing © Farlex 2012]

----

epi- = elephant happy (smiling)
following = after

Story

The elephants were happily following each other

Term Use

epidemic = occurring suddenly in numbers clearly in excess of normal
expectancy
[Dorland's Medical Dictionary for Health Consumers. © 2007 by Saunders]

exo- = xo (love)
outside = outdoors

Story

She loved (X's and O's) being outdoors

Term Use

exotoxin = a toxin that is secreted or excreted by a living microorganism
[Mosby's Medical Dictionary, 9th edition. © 2009, Elsevier.]

----

fore- = forehead
front = fro on front side

Story

Fro was growing on the front side of his head on his forehead

Term Use

forearm = the portion of the upper extremity between the elbow and the wrist
[Mosby's Medical Dictionary, 9th edition. © 2009, Elsevier.]

hyper- = hat on viper
beyond = bee beyond joy

Story

Viper with hat was very energetic after a bee stung it

Term Use

hyperalkalinity = A condition of excessive alkalinity
[Medical Dictionary, © 2009 Farlex and Partners]

----

hypo = hippo
under = going under

Story

Hippo went under the water

Term Use

hypodontia = A congenital or acquired condition of having fewer than the normal complement of teeth
[Farlex Partner Medical Dictionary © Farlex 2012]

in- = Native American Indian
not = knot

Story

Native American Indian tying a knot

Term Use

incurable = Denoting a disease or morbid process unresponsive to medical or surgical treatment.
[Farlex Partner Medical Dictionary © Farlex 2012]

----

infra- = infrared
situated beneath = below something

Story

Infrared cat was below the table

Term Use

infratemporal= Below the temporal fossa of the skull.
[Medical Dictionary, © 2009 Farlex and Partners]

inter- = inner-tube
occurring between = in the between

Story

He was in between two inner tubes

Term Use

intercalary = Occurring, or interposed, between parts.
[Collins Dictionary of Medicine © Robert M. Youngson, 2005]

----

intra- = in truck
situated within = inside

Story

He was inside of the truck

Term Use

intrabronchial= Within the bronchi or bronchial tubes.
[Farlex Partner Medical Dictionary © Farlex 2012]

meso - = messy mice
middle = in the middle with a mitt

Story

In the middle of their cage, the mice made a mess with their mitts

Term Use

mesoderm = The middle embryonic germ layer, lying between the ectoderm and the endoderm, from which connective tissue, muscle, bone, and the urogenital and circulatory systems develop.
[American Heritage® Dictionary of the English Language, Fifth Edition. © 2011]

----

meta- = mat
later in time = ladder with clock

Story

Used a ladder on a mat to reach the clock up above

Term Use

metestrus = The period following estrus in most female mammals, when the corpus luteum begins to form.
[American Heritage® Dictionary of the English Language, Fifth Edition. © 2011]

opistho- = a pistol
rear = rear behind (butt)

Story

A pistol shot him in the rear end

Term Use

opisthomi = An order of eel-like fishes having the scapular arch attached to the vertebrae, but not connected with the skull
[Webster's Revised Unabridged Dictionary. © 1913]

----

pachy- = back pack
thick = thick

Story

The back pack was very thick because of all of the books inside of it

Term Use

pachyderm = any of various large, thick-skinned mammals, such as the elephant, rhinoceros, or hippopotamus
[American Heritage® Dictionary of the English Language, Fifth Edition. © 2011]

para- = parachute
disordered = disco ball ordered

Story

The guy was in midair with his parachute as he ordered a disco ball online

Term Use

paranoia = a condition characterized by an elaborate, overly suspicious system of thinking. It often includes delusions of persecution and grandeur usually centered on one major theme
[Mosby's Medical Dictionary, 9th edition. © 2009, Elsevier.]

----

per- = parrot
completely = (honey)comb + plate

Story

Parrot completely ate the honeycomb off its plate

Term Use

perfuse = To force or instill (fluids) into an organ or a vessel.
[Medical Dictionary, © 2009 Farlex and Partners]

platy- = platypus
flatness = wide and thin

Story

The platypus was wide and flat while swimming

Term Use
platymeric = having a broad femur
[Farlex Partner Medical Dictionary © Farlex 2012]

----

post- = postage stamp
behind = on the other side

Story

I accidently put the postage stamp on the other side of the envelope

Term Use
postcardial = Behind the heart.
[Medical Dictionary, © 2009 Farlex and Partners]

pre- = preach
anterior = anteater

Story

Anteater preaching

Term Use

predormitum = The stage of decreasing consciousness that represents a transition stage between wakefulness and sleep.
[Farlex Partner Medical Dictionary © Farlex 2012]

----

pseudo- = sewing dough
false = flask

Story

The sewing dough was sewing together a flask but it looked fake

Term Use

pseudocyst = A cyst the wall of which is formed by a host cell and not by a parasite.
[Farlex Partner Medical Dictionary © Farlex 2012]

re- = reed (clarinet)
again = repeat

Story

Using the reed, the clarinet player kept repeating the same song

Term Use
rejuvenation = the restoration of youthful health and vitality.
[Mosby's Medical Dictionary, 9th edition. © 2009, Elsevier.]

----

semi- = semi truck
half = cut in half

Story

The semi truck was cut in half

Term Use
semisupine = pertaining to a posture that is between a midposition and the supine position.
[Mosby's Medical Dictionary, 9th edition. © 2009, Elsevier.]

sub- = subway (train)
beneath = underneath

Story

The subway could only run underneath on the city tracks

Term Use
subungual = beneath a fingernail or toenail.
[Mosby's Medical Dictionary, 9th edition. © 2009, Elsevier.]

----

super- = superhero
above = flying above showing abs

Story

Superhero was flying above everyone while showing his abs

Term Use
supernatant = situated above or on top of something.
[Mosby's Medical Dictionary, 9th edition. © 2009, Elsevier.]

syn- = sink
together = glued together

Story

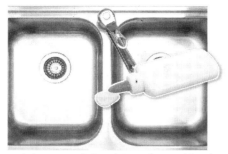

The sinks were joined together with glue

Term Use
synthetic = pertaining to a substance that is produced by an artificial rather than a natural process or material.
[Mosby's Medical Dictionary, 9th edition. © 2009, Elsevier.]

----

tauto- = taco + toe
same = duplicate

Story

The chef made 2 tacos with toes, and they all looked the same

Term Use
tautomeral = pertaining to certain neurons that send processes to the white matter on the same side of the spinal cord
[Medical Dictionary, © 2009 Farlex and Partners]

trans- = transit bus + tree
through = going through

Story

The transit bus went through the tree

Term Use
transplacental = Crossing the placenta.
[Farlex Partner Medical Dictionary © Farlex 2012]

----

ultra- = umbrella on a truck
excess = excess power pulling an X

Story

Truck with an umbrella excessively pulling an X

Term Use
ultrasound= Sound having a frequency greater than 30,000 Hz.
[Farlex Partner Medical Dictionary © Farlex 2012]

xero- = xylophone in the shape of a zero
dryness = desert

Story

The xylophone shaped like a zero was in the desert and somehow it was
so dry that you couldn't play it

Term Use
xerophthalmia = a condition of dry and lusterless corneas and
conjunctival areas, usually the result of vitamin A deficiency and
associated with night blindness
[Mosby's Medical Dictionary, 9th edition. © 2009, Elsevier.]

----

zygo- = zebra and a goat
yoke = egg yolk

Story

Zebra and Goat were eating egg yolks

Term Use
zygogenesis = the formation of a zygote.
[Mosby's Medical Dictionary, 9th edition. © 2009, Elsevier.]

Section III

SUFFIXES

SUFFIXES

Just like prefixes, we combine the images that created for suffix and meaning in order to come up with a story.

Memory Tip:

Remember to Review as you go through these stories.

-algia = algae
pain = feeling pain

Story

The algae was in deep pain after being split open

Term Use
epigastralgia = pain in the epigastric region
[Farlex Partner Medical Dictionary © Farlex 2012]

-ase = ace of diamond (card)
enzyme = angel slime

Story

The angel won all the slime after having all aces in poker

Term Use
luciferase = An enzyme present in the cells of bioluminescent organisms
that catalyzes the oxidation of luciferin and ATP, producing light.
[The American Heritage® Medical Dictionary. © 2007. Houghton Mifflin Company]

-blastoma = bazooka blast
tumor of cells = turmeric on cells

Story

bazooka was blasting turmeric on the cells

Term Use

archiblastoma = a tumor composed of cells derived from the layer of tissue surrounding the germinal vesicle.
[Mosby's Medical Dictionary, 9th edition. © 2009, Elsevier.]

-cyte = eye sight (glasses)
cell = cell phone

Story

I was looking at the cells in my cell phone with my eye glasses on

Term Use

Leukocyte = white blood cell
[American Heritage® Dictionary of the English Language, 5th Edition. © 2011. Houghton Mifflin Harcourt Publishing Company]

-derma = door + mouse
skin = skin

Story

The door had all of the skin that the hairless mouse was shedding over the years

Term Use

chyloderma = Lymph accumulated in the enlarged lymphatic vessels and thickened skin of the scrotum.
[Medical Dictionary, © 2009 Farlex and Partners]

-desis = dentist
binding = binding together

Story

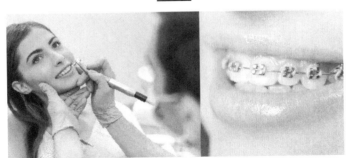

The dentist was binding the teeth together with braces

Term Use

fasciodesis = Surgical attachment of a fascia to another fascia or a tendon.
[Farlex Partner Medical Dictionary © Farlex 2012]

-ectomy = egg + tummy
removal of anatomical structure = <-the action

Story

The egg had the tummy removed which was stuck since birth

Term Use
phlecbectomy = excision of a segment of a vein, performed sometimes for the cure of varicose veins
[Farlex Partner Medical Dictionary © Farlex 2012]

-edem = EDM (music)
swelling due to fluid = getting bigger

Story

All of the youngsters at the EDM show got swollen because of all the raving they did that night

Term Use
cephaledema = a swelling of the brain caused by fluid accumulation
[Mosby's Medical Dictionary, 9th edition. © 2009, Elsevier.]

-esthesia = anesthesia
feeling = feeling numb

Story

The anesthesia made her not feel any pain during surgery

Term Use
hypercryesthesia = extreme sensibility to cold
[Farlex Partner Medical Dictionary © Farlex 2012]

-gen = gem
generates = generator

Story

Gem was attached to a generator because of all of the power it was
giving out

Term Use
aerogen = A gas-forming microorganism.
[Farlex Partner Medical Dictionary © Farlex 2012]

-globin = globe
containing protein = protein powder

Story

The globe was working out so it took extra protein to get buff

Term Use
hemoglobin = The protein in the red blood cells of vertebrates that carries oxygen from the lungs to tissues and that consists of four polypeptide subunits, each of which is bound to an iron-containing heme molecule.
[The American Heritage® Medical Dictionary. 2007. Houghton Mifflin Company]

-graph = graph paper
something written = writing with pencil

Story

She used graph paper to sketch out her drawing with a pencil of the house she was designing

Term Use
radiograph = A negative image on photographic film made by exposure to x-rays or gamma rays that have passed through matter or tissue.
[Farlex Partner Medical Dictionary © Farlex 2012]

-helminth = helmet
worm = worm

Story

Worm wearing a helmet

Term Use

platyhelminth = Common name for any flatworm of the phylum Platyhelminthes; any cestode (tapeworm) or trematode (fluke).
[Farlex Partner Medical Dictionary © Farlex 2012]

-itis = an eye test
inflammation = being inflamed and fire coming out

Story

As she was taking the eye test, it started to get inflamed and get larger with fire coming out of her eyes

Term Use

sarcitis = inflammation of muscle tissue
[Medical Dictionary, © 2009 Farlex and Partners]

-kinesis = cane + sister
movement = moving

Story

The cane helped my sister move around the house

Term Use
lymphokinpesis = Circulation of lymph in the lymphatic vessels and through the lymph nodes.
[Farlex Partner Medical Dictionary © Farlex 2012]

-lapse = running laps
a slip = slipping

Story

As the runner was running laps, he slipped and fell backwards

Term Use
collapse = A condition of extreme prostration, similar or identical to hypovolemic shock and due to the same causes.
[Farlex Partner Medical Dictionary © Farlex 2012]

-lepsy = lips
a seizure = having a seizure

Story

The lips were moving so fast that they began to have a seizure

Term Use

epilepsy = A chronic disorder characterized by paroxysmal brain dysfunction due to excessive neuronal discharge, and usually associated with some alteration of consciousness.
[Medical Dictionary for the Health Professions and Nursing © Farlex 2012]

-logy = lodge
science = beakers and magnifying glass

Story

He built the camping lodge out of beakers and a magnifying glass

Term Use

neonatology = the diagnosis and treatment of disorders of the newborn.
[Dorland's Medical Dictionary for Health Consumers. © 2007 by Saunders, Elsevier, Inc]

-lucent = loop cent (penny)
light admitting = flashlight

Story

A loop made of cents turning on a flashlight

Term Use
radiolucent = Relatively penetrable by x-rays or other forms of radiation.
[Farlex Partner Medical Dictionary © Farlex 2012]

-mania = Wrestlemania wrestler + mind
abnormal love for = huge heart

Story

Man was at Wrestlemania on the mind was wrestling with a huge heart

Term Use
arithmomania = a morbid impulse to count
[Farlex Partner Medical Dictionary © Farlex 2012]

-meter = parking meter
measuing = measuring tape

Story

Measuring the parking meter with a measuring tape

Term Use

scopometer = an instrument for measuring the density of a suspension
[Medical Dictionary, © 2009 Farlex and Partners]

-mnesia = money she (girl)
memory = SD Memory Card

Story

Money rich girl bought a huge SD memory card

Term Use

amnesia = A disturbance in the memory of stored information of very variable durations, minutes to months, in contrast to short-term memory, manifest by total or partial inability, to recall past experiences
[Farlex Partner Medical Dictionary © Farlex 2012]

-motor = motor (engine)
effects of activity in a body part = all body parts moving

Story

A person was moving and shaking all of their body parts while on top of a motor

Term Use
visceromotor = pertaining to nerve impulses that control visceral smooth muscle
[Mosby's Medical Dictionary, 9th edition. © 2009, Elsevier.]

-ole = orange pole
small = small

Story

Small orange colored pole

Term Use
arteriole = A small terminal branch of an artery
[Collins Dictionary of Medicine © Robert M. Youngson 2004, 2005]

-opia = orange peeing
visual condition = eye balls

Story

Orange peeing on eye balls

Term Use

senopia = an improvement in the near vision of the aged caused by the myopia associated with increasing lenticular nuclear sclerosis.
[Mosby's Medical Dictionary, 9th edition. © 2009, Elsevier.]

-opsy = hops + sink
examination = magnifying glass

Story

Magnifying glass hops over to the sink

Term Use

autopsy = a postmortem examination performed to confirm or determine the cause of death.
[Mosby's Dental Dictionary, 2nd edition. © 2008 Elsevier, Inc.]

-orexia = boat oar as an X
appetite = eating

Story

Using boat oars in the shape of an x to eat fish

Term Use

dysorexia = Diminished or perverted appetite.
[Farlex Partner Medical Dictionary © Farlex 2012]

-osmia = house milk
sense of smell = nose

Story

She squirted milk out of nose on to the house

Term Use

merosmia = A condition in which the perception of certain odors is wanting; olfactory dysfunction analogous to color blindness.
[Farlex Partner Medical Dictionary © Farlex 2012]

-otia = tea bag in the shape of a circle
ear = ear

Story

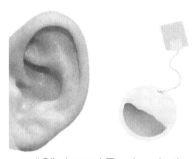

Dipping an "O" shaped Tea bag in the ear

Term Use

microtia = Smallness of the auricle of the ear with a blind or absent external acoustic meatus.
[Farlex Partner Medical Dictionary © Farlex 2012]

-phon = phone
sound = music

Story

Playing music on the phone

Term Use

autophony = Increased hearing of one's own voice, breath sounds, arterial murmurs, and other noises of the upper body
[Farlex Partner Medical Dictionary © Farlex 2012]

-phor = Ford truck
carrier = carrying in the back

Story

The back of the Ford truck was carrying a car

Term Use

physaliphore = A mother cell, or giant cell containing a large vacuole, in a malignant growth.
[Farlex Partner Medical Dictionary © Farlex 2012]

-pnea = knee + apple
breathing = oxygen mask

Story

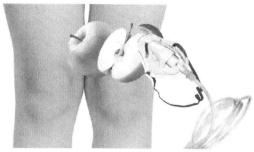

The knee put on an oxygen mask connected to the apple in order to breath

Term Use

dyspnea = a distressful subjective sensation of uncomfortable breathing that may be caused by many disorders, including certain heart and respiratory conditions, strenuous exercise, or anxiety.
[Mosby's Medical Dictionary, 9th edition. © 2009, Elsevier.]

-ptosis = peanut butter toast
sinking down = falling

Story

Peanut butter toast fell down as you were eating it

Term Use

esophagoptosis = Relaxation and downward displacement of the walls of the esophagus.
[Farlex Partner Medical Dictionary © Farlex 2012]

-rrhag = rag
excessive flow = flowing water

Story

Rag was used to clean the flow of excess water coming out of the faucet

Term Use

metrorrhagia = Any irregular, acyclic bleeding from the uterus between periods.
[Farlex Partner Medical Dictionary © Farlex 2012]

-scope = Scope mouthwash
instrument for observation = telescope

Story

The telescope was used to look at a bottle of Scope mouthwash

Term Use

ciliariscope = An instrument for examining the ciliary region of the eye.
[Medical Dictionary, © 2009 Farlex and Partners]

-stroma = strobe lights + mouse
supporting tissue of an organ = tissues on organ (music)

Story

The strobe lights made the mouse go crazy and it place tissues all over the organ

Term Use
myostroma = The supporting connective tissue or framework of muscular tissue.
[Farlex Partner Medical Dictionary © Farlex 2012]

-tripsy = tripping
to crush = crushing

Story

Tripping over crushed asphalt

Term Use
sarcotripsy = Rarely used term for use of a crushing forceps to stop hemorrhage.
[Farlex Partner Medical Dictionary © Farlex 2012]

-trophy = trophy
growth = growing

Story

The trophy just kept growing as it kept getting fed

Term Use
lipotrophy = An increase of fat in the body.
[Farlex Partner Medical Dictionary © Farlex 2012]

-uria = urine + apple
presence of a substance in the urine = cup with urine

Story

There were apple slices floating in the cup of urine

Term Use
enzymuria = the presence of enzymes in urine.
[Mosby's Medical Dictionary, 9th edition. © 2009, Elsevier.]

Section IV

ROOT WORDS

ROOT WORDS

Here are some root words with stories to help you memorize them.

Memory Tip:

Our body and our brain is composed primarily of water. Many times, when we're feeling tired or unfocused, it's because we are dehydrated or on the verge of being dehydrated. We need to constantly keep ourselves hydrated by drinking a lot of water.

So make sure to always keep a glass or your bottle of water near you to keep yourself moving forward.

adip/o = a dip
fat, fatty = blob of fat

Story

A dip of blob of fat

Term Use

adipocele = a hernia containing fat or fatty tissue
[Mosby's Medical Dictionary, 9th edition. © 2009, Elsevier.]

----

anter/o = ant eater
front = front + frying pan

Story

The ant eater is hitting the front of his belly with a frying pan

Term Use

anterolateral = In front and away from the middle line.
[Farlex Partner Medical Dictionary © Farlex 2012]

aut/o = automobile
self = checking out in mirror

Story

Checking yourself out in your auto's mirror

Term Use

autism = mental disorder in which language and social and relational skills are undeveloped. Individuals can be abnormally socially withdrawn.
[Jonas: Mosby's Dictionary of Complementary and Alternative Medicine. (c) 2005, Elsevier.]

----

blenn/o = blender
mucus = boogers

Story

Blender is blending boogers

Term Use

blennogenic = Producing or secreting mucus.
[Farlex Partner Medical Dictionary © Farlex 2012]

bucc/o = buccaneer pirate
cheek = cheek

Story

Buccaneer pirate punched another pirate in the cheek

Term Use
Anorexia = a fold of fatty tissue, literally a "little cheek" beneath the chin.
Also called double chin.
[Mosby's Medical Dictionary, 9th edition. © 2009, Elsevier.]
----

caud/o = cauldron
tail = tail

Story

Witch was making tail soup in cauldron

Term Use
caudate = Tailed; possessing a tail.
[Farlex Partner Medical Dictionary © Farlex 2012]

dacry/o = dog crying
tears = tears

Story

Dog was crying as tears were running down its face

Term Use
dacryorrhea = An excessive secretion of tears.
[Farlex Partner Medical Dictionary © Farlex 2012]

----

dynamo = dynamite + domino
power or strength = strong muscles

Story

The dynamite blow up the dominoes on the guy's strong arms

Term Use
dynamogenesis = The production of force, especially of muscular or nervous energy.
[Farlex Partner Medical Dictionary © Farlex 2012]

hepat/o = hepa filter
liver = liver

Story

Cleaning the hepa filter with a piece of liver

Term Use
hepatitis = Inflammation of the liver; usually from a viral infection, a drug, or toxic agent.
[Medical Dictionary for the Health Professions and Nursing © Farlex 2012]

----

kary/o = carry
nucleus of a cell = nuclear bomb on cell phone

Story

I was carrying a nuclear bomb on top of a cell phone

Term Use
karyoplastin = The achromatic nuclear material that forms the spindle apparatus.
[Farlex Partner Medical Dictionary © Farlex 2012]

lepid/o = leopard
flake or scale = fish scale

Story

Leopard was playing fish's scales

Term Use

lepidosis = Any scaly or desquamating eruption such as pityriasis.
[Medical Dictionary, © 2009 Farlex and Partners]

----

leuk/o = lake
white = white blanket

Story

Placed a white blanket over the lake

Term Use

leukemia = Progressive proliferation of abnormal leukocytes (white blood cells) found in hemopoietic tissues, other organs, and usually in the blood in increased numbers.
[Farlex Partner Medical Dictionary © Farlex 2012]

mamm/o = memo-pad
breast = breast

Story

She drew breast on the memo-pad

Term Use

mammiform = Resembling a breast; breast-shaped.
[Farlex Partner Medical Dictionary © Farlex 2012]

----

nas/o = nos tank
nose = nose

Story

Nos tank blowing inside of the nose

Term Use

nasociliary = Relating to the nose and eyelids
[Farlex Partner Medical Dictionary © Farlex 2012]

nephr/o = net + afro
kidney = kidney beans

Story

Catching kidney beans with a net on the afro

Term Use
nephrogenetic = Developing into kidney tissue.
[Farlex Partner Medical Dictionary © Farlex 2012]

----

odont/o = hula hoop dentist
teeth = tooth

Story

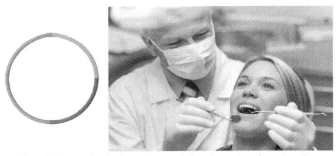

Dentist was hula hooping while cleaning her teeth

Term Use
odontopathy = Any disease of the teeth or of their sockets.
[Farlex Partner Medical Dictionary © Farlex 2012]

palpebral = pepper + bra
eyelid = eyelid

Story

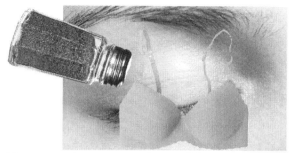

She poured pepper on the eyelid and caught it with a bra

Term Use

palpebral reflex = the eyelids close when the eyelids are touched.
[Farlex Partner Medical Dictionary © Farlex 2012]

----

pil/o = pill
hair = hair

Story

Pills were stuck all along his hair

Term Use

pilomotor = Moving the hair
[Farlex Partner Medical Dictionary © Farlex 2012]

acchar/o = sack
sugar = sugar

Story

Sack of sugar

Term Use

saccharoid = Having a texture similar to that of granulated sugar. Used of rocks and minerals.

[American Heritage® Dictionary of the English Language, 5th Edition. Copyright © 2011, Houghton Mifflin Harcourt Publishing Company.]

----

spir/o = spiral
coil = coil

Story

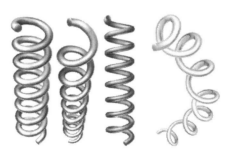

The coil was a spiracle shape

Term Use

spiradenitis = A funiculus beginning in the coil of a sweat gland.
[Medical Dictionary, © 2009 Farlex and Partners]

steth/o = stethoscope
chest = chest

Story

Hearing the heartbeat by placing the stethoscope on her chest

Term Use
stethometer = an instrument for measuring the circular dimension or expansion of the chest.
[Dorland's Medical Dictionary for Health Consumers. © 2007 by Saunders, Elsevier, Inc.]

----

succ/o = sucking with straw
juice = juice box

Story

Sucking from the juice box with a straw

Term Use
succagogue = Stimulating the flow of juice.
[Farlex Partner Medical Dictionary © Farlex 2012]

tephr/o = volcanic tephra
gray = ash colored

Story

The volcanic tephra was a gray ashy color

Term Use
tephromalacia = Softening of the gray matter of the brain or spinal cord.
[Farlex Partner Medical Dictionary © Farlex 2012]

----

thromb/o = trombone
blood clot = blood bag

Story

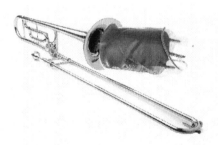

The trombone had a bag of blood stuck in it

Term Use
thromboarteritis = arterial inflammation with thrombus formation.
[Mosby's Medical Dictionary, 9th edition. © 2009, Elsevier.]

tors/o = Taurus (bull)
twisted = horns twisted

Story

The Taurus were head butting each other and had their horns twisted together

Term Use

torsiversion = A malposition of a tooth in which it is rotated on its long axis.
[Medical Dictionary for the Health Professions and Nursing © Farlex 2012]

Section V

SCIENCE TERMS

TOP SCIENCE TERMS

Here are some of the top science terms from different subjects, Abbreviations, Biology, Microbiology, Genetics, Chemistry, Bio Chemistry, Microbiology, First Aid, Pathology, Psychology, Neurology, and more.

Abbreviation/Acronyms

MP = Mop

Mentoposterior Position = Mint + Post + Magician

Story

Mop cleaning a mint on the person's back which has a long post sticking out of it while a magician was holding it

----

Abbreviation/Acronyms

FX = Fax machine

Fracture = break

Story

Fractured the Fax machine by breaking a piece off of it

Abbreviation
MCL = MC (rapper) LL Cool J
Medial Collateral Ligament = Medal + Collar + Licking Mint

Story

MC LL Cool J won a medal for licking mint off of a collar

Abbreviation
DNA = Dinner Plate
Deoxyribonucleic Acid = Dog + Oxygen + Rib + Nuclear Acid

Story

Dog ate the dinner plate and needed oxygen to breath. It had food stuck
in his ribs and needed nuclear acid to melt it away

Biology

Glucose : A monosaccharide sugar, C6H12O6, that is used by living things to obtain energy through the process of aerobic respiration within cells. It is the principal circulating sugar in the blood of humans and other mammals.

Story

Glue shut close a case full of sugar.

If you want to remember C6H12O6, you can combine your images with numbers to the letters.

C = Car | 6 = Sticks. H = Hand | 12 = Dozen. O = Orange | 6 = Sticks

Story

A car made of Sugar and is full of sticks runs over a Hand holding a dozen eggs and out comes Oranges full of more sticks inside.

Biology
Chlorophyll = Chlorine + Fill Gas Pump
The green plant pigment = Green

Story

Filled up a plant with green chlorine using the gas pump

Cellular Biology
Ribosomes = the site of protein synthesis in the cell by linking amino acids into chains.

Story

Rib s'mores with minnow fish were linked together like a chain and wrapped around a protein shake

Cellular Biology

Mitochondria = An organelle of the cell cytoplasm consisting of two sets of membranes, a smooth continuous outer coat and an inner membrane arranged in tubules or more often in folds that form plate-like double membranes called cristae;

mitochondria are the principal energy source of the cell and contain the cytochrome enzymes of terminal electron transport and the enzymes of the citric acid cycle, fatty acid oxidation, and oxidative phosphorylation.

Story

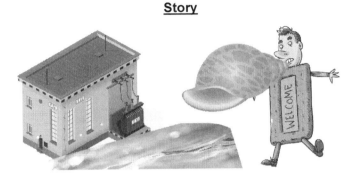

Mat blew a conch to dry out the water coming out of the powerhouse full of batteries

Chemistry

Ion : an atom or group of atoms that has acquired an electrical charge through the gain or loss of an electron or electrons.

Story

Eye flicked on the light switch which caused the electricity to turn on

---

Chemistry

Proton : A positively charged particle located in the nucleus of an atom of an element, the number of which governs its chemical properties.

Story

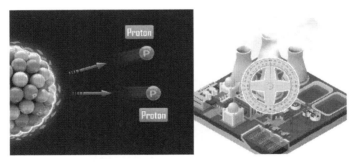

Protractor in the shape of a cross weighed a ton as it was placed in the middle of a nuclear power plant

Neuroscience

Neurogenesis : Formation of the nervous system or formation of neurons within the adult brain.

Story

Neuron growing on a gem with sauce being poured over it. All of this was on top of a brain.

Pathology

Analgesia (analgesic) : the absence of pain; removing pain.

Sometimes the best stories are the ones that are a little bit more graphic. Also, you are a medical student so this next story shouldn't shock you.

Story

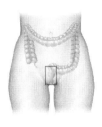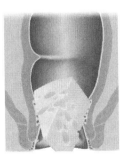

The anal canal was stuffed with cheese and the person didn't feel any pain

Psychology

Psychosis : any major mental disorder of organic or emotional origin marked by derangement of personality and loss of contact with reality, with delusions and hallucinations and often with incoherent speech, disorganized and agitated behavior, or illusions.

Story

Cyclops with little sister were in an insane asylum because they were going crazy

ANATOMY

I put together a series of books to help you memorize every single part of the human anatomical body structure.
Go to AnatomyMasteryBook.com to learn more.

In the memory competitions that I compete in, we have an event called abstract images. It's pretty self-explanatory, and all that we do is memorize the order of random crazy shaped abstract images.

It looks something like this:

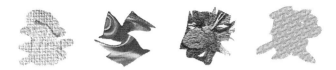

The way that we memorize the order of these abstract images, is by creating a story. What a shocker right?

So the first one in this series would be a Ballerina dancing with a Boot being worn by an Octopus on top of a Metal plate.

Now that you know we do that, we're going to take a similar approach to linking the terms used to label the different parts of the human body.

Let's jump right in.

Skeletal System
Scapula = scalpel

Story

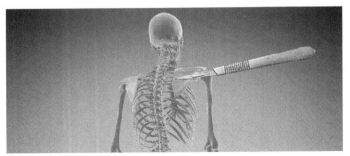

Scrapping pieces off of your scapula

Skeletal System
Femur = fever + mirror

Story

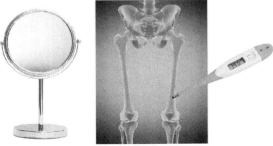

Your thigh starts burning up as the femur bone inside of it gets a fever
after it looks at itself in the mirror

Muscular System
Deltoid = Del Taco + Toy

Story

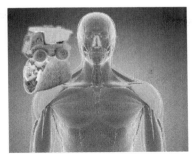

Del Taco had a toy inside of it and poured all of its contents on the deltoid

---

Nervous System
Cerebellum = Celery + Bell

Story

Growing celery on the cerebellum every time the bell chimes

Term meaning
The Cerebellum is the part of the brain at the back of the skull in vertebrates. Its function is to coordinate and regulate muscular activity.

Lymphatic system
Spleen : spoon leaning

Story

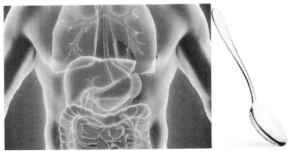

Spoon was leaning on the spleen as it removed blood from it

Term meaning
The spleen is an abdominal organ involved in the production and removal of blood cells in most vertebrates and forming part of the immune system.

Circulatory System
Pleura = Pluto the dog roaring

Story

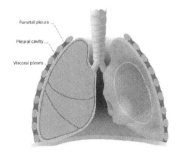

Pluto was roaring to clear up his lungs

Term Meaning
each of a pair of serous membranes lining the thorax and enveloping the lungs in humans and other mammals.

Respiratory System
Trachea = Trix cereal

Story

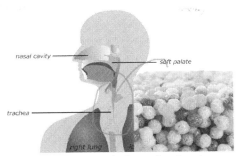

Flicking Trix cereal along the trachea

Term Meaning
The trachea is a wide, hollow tube that connects the larynx (or voice box) to the bronchi of the lungs.
[www.innerbody.com]

Urinary System/Renal
Bladder = batter

Story

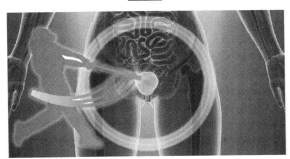

The batter hit the bladder full of urine

Term Meaning
The Bladder is a membranous sac in humans and other animals, in which urine is collected for excretion.

Digestive System/ Gastrointestinal (GI)

Liver = leaf + hair

Story

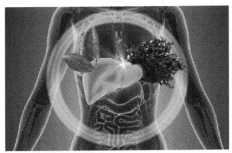

The leafy hair was growing on the liver as it helped speed up her
metabolism

Term Meaning

The Liver is a large lobed glandular organ in the abdomen of vertebrates,
involved in many metabolic processes.

Reproductive System

Testicle : Test + icicle

Story

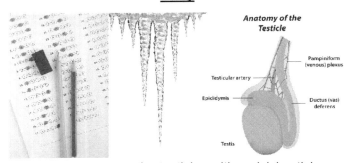

Taking a test on the testicles with an icicle stick

Term Meaning

the male gonad or reproductive gland, either of two oval glands located
in the scrotum.

Endocrine System

Better Memory Now

Pineal Gland = peanut oil + golf land

Story

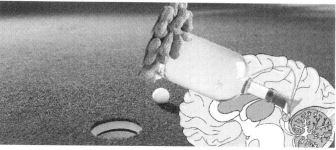

Pouring peanut oil on the pineal gland while playing golf on the big piece of land

Term Use
The Pineal Gland is a pea-sized conical mass of tissue behind the third ventricle of the brain, secreting a hormone-like substance in some mammals

THANK YOU

Thank you for going through the
Medical Terminology Mastery Book!

Remember to get your free Continued Education gift at:
www.MedTermsBook.com/Master

Remember that your purchase allows you to download the
Full Colored Kindle Version of this book for Free! Get it today
at Amazon and please leave us a review on the page when
you get the chance!

Look forward to meeting you one day and hearing all about
your success story!

Take care,

Luis Angel

LEARN MORE/CONTACT

Learn more about Luis Angel's "**Better Memory Now**" programs and other Memory Training material for Professionals, Students, Memory Athletes, and Everyone Else, by going to:

www.AEMind.com

SOCIAL

YT: Youtube.com/aemindmemory
FB: Facebook.com/aemind1
IG: ae.mind
Twitter: @aemind
SnapChat: aemind

Printed in Great Britain
by Amazon